Sunshine Everyday

SUNSHINE EVERYDAY

Sharon Thames

DEDICATION

This book is dedicated to Ruthie Johnson, Fred Hillery and James Thomas, thank you for inspiring, encouraging, and believing in me.

CONTENTS

HOLIDAYS

BIRTHDAY WISHES

REFLECTIONS

Sunshine Everyday is a compilation of poems written in different categories to inspire, encourage, reminisce and think on through life's ups and downs, struggles, disappointments, accomplishments, and relationships as it reflects on how you can still find sunshine through the rain. Enjoy the readings.

INSPIRATION & ENCOURAGEMENT

A SMILE

They often say a smile is worth a thousand words,

Whether it is big or small in style,

It's still the loveliest we've observed.

A smile brightens the day as often as it unfolds,

Lifting spirits across the way,

That's what we've always been told.

It doesn't cost anything to smile all day long.

A smile has such a ring, like words to a favorite song.

So, go ahead and smile, lifting spirits everywhere,

Even across the miles, it will be seen from a glare.

A CONTAGIOUS CHRISTIAN

Lord, hear my cry and accept my plea,

For a contagious Christian, I want to be.

I know this role entails a lot,

But everything I need I know, You've got.

Help me to understand it's not about me,

That the bigger picture involves unity.

Help me to do Your will, even in things I can't see,

Because You've already proven, You're trustworthy.

Help me with wisdom only You can give,

That would enhance my horizons as I live.

Guide my tongue every time I speak,

Keep it strong even when I'm weak.

Lord, continue to mold and stretch me out,

So everyone can see what Christianity is all about.

This is my prayer; I surrender to You,

Let the glory be Yours in everything I do.

Amen

A DESTINED WOMAN

Sometimes in life, as we start to juggle, our focus takes on wings,

Puts us in a place of struggle, and we become confused about everything.

We go from day to day, neglecting to read God's word,

Continuing in our own way because His voice we have not heard.

Yet, deep inside, we realize this life is not our own,

We are here for a purpose and have not been left alone.

We should lean not to our own understanding,

But in all our ways, keep God in common

Because it is through Him that you, become a Destined Woman.

A POEM OF GRATITUDE

Oh, heavenly Father, I'm Your biggest fan.

Thank You for waking me once again.

Even though I am physically and emotionally drained,

It's because of You that I am not insane.

Now keep me in your shelter, where I am the most safe.

So when life distractions happen, it will not move me out of place.

Amen.

A POEM OF PRAISE

Our Father, whom art in heaven.

Hallowed be thy name.

I come to thee with praise in me pleading humbly.

Thanking You and lifting You up, putting my trust in thee,

faithfully, continually, for reigning down on me.

You are my shepherd; I shall not want.

You're my beginning, and my end,

My all and all, my confidant, my savior, and my friend.

With all that is within me, I give thee all the praise,

All the glory, and the honor, until my dying days!

CHANGE

What is it about change that we struggle with in life?

And why is it that change always brings about strife?

What is it about change that we're slow to accept?

Is it because we're unaware the deepness of its depth?

What is it about change that tends to make us weary?

And why is it with change, we always want to be leery?

What is it about change that causes us to fear?

And why do we choose to keep change way back in the rear?

What is it about change that turns us inside out?

And why is it with change, at first, we always doubt?

What is it about change?

It happens whether we want it to or not,

And to choose to live without it is not part of the plot.

SHARON THAMES

What is it about change that when it does appear,

We do accept the change and hold it very dear?

HIGHER GROUND

In times of despair and troubles all around,

Lord, help me to remember the purpose of higher ground.

IN THE VALLEY

I will walk through the valley regardless of how it feels,

Looking to my help which cometh from the hills.

For God is my refuge when the enemy attacks,

No weapon will prosper because He's got my back!

MY PRAYER

Lord, I stretch my hands to thee,

For more prayerful would I like to be.

You are my strength from day to day,

And prayer is what's needed to guide the way.

So often I neglect to fall upon my knees,

To thank You, to praise You, for fulfilling all my needs.

You keep me in the shelter of Your loving arms,

And in the midst of all Your great loving charm.

Lord, You do all these things so gracefully,

And prayer would keep more peace in me.

So humbly I come, and faithfully I believe,

For if I'm more prayerful, in me will You be pleased?

SUNSHINE
EVERYDAY

How can you have sunshine every day even when it rains,

still have sunshine come your way?

Sunshine is not too bright that it can't always shine through.

It doesn't always have to come from others; it can come from you.

So, when your days are gloomy, and the fog keeps rolling in,

Lift your head a moment and see what happens then.

For if you listen closely, you will hear Him say,

"If you keep your eye on Me, you can have sunshine every day!

WHEN YOU'RE
FEELING BLUE

Life is full of challenges; it's full of struggles, too.

But there is someone bigger who will always see you through.

His name is Jesus, Jehovah, too.

King of kings and Lord of lords are only just a few.

He freshens the air and sends the rain,

He knows just how to ease your pain.

He's a delicious taste to the very last drop,

Makes your cup runneth over, and puts the lolli in your pop.

He will pick you up, never let you down,

Give you a different outlook all around.

So, on those days when you're feeling blue and feel like giving in,

Keep the faith and hold to the fact that your brokenness, He is sure to mend!

FRIENDS

I've often wondered why I fought so hard to be,

Accepted and to fit in with everyone around me.

I never caused a problem with anyone therein,

And I only needed one of them to really be my friend.

I never knew what it was like to hang with two or three,

And get along with everyone. I never thought it could be.

As I grew older, becoming a bit more wise,

I found myself still searching for friends about my size.

But since my walk with Jesus, my friends are no more few,

I don't worry about fitting in, and I have more than one or two.

So, my advice I have for all who are seeking friends,

All you need to do is just let Jesus in!

LOVE & ROMANCE

A HOLLOW LOVE

From the first day we met, who would have ever known,

How deep a love for you would rapidly have grown?

Yes, I've had my share of life's hurt and pain,

Yet, I sit and wait for the day your love I'll gain.

In many ways you tried to show a love that seemed sincere,

but somehow it always found a way to fade and disappear.

I do not know what causes you to have such change of heart,

And every time you do, it catches me off guard.

Then we flip the script and settle for being friends.

When I continue reaching out, you accuse me of trying again.

Maybe it's best to just let bygones be,

Cause even if nothing else, being friends should come naturally.

I don't know why it's hard for us to be close and free.

Is it because you don't have that depth of love for me?

I wish that with it all and everything we've shared,

Being nothing but friends would show you really cared.

But it's okay if being friends just really don't appeal,

Because in due time, one thing I know this ole heart will heal!

A NEW LOVE

When we first met, it was like a dream come true.

I was so captivated by your looks; I didn't know what to do.

You asked me on a date and had me with your smile.

I knew right then, without a doubt, I really liked your style.

That's when my whole life changed, starting me with a new tomorrow.

It was then and there I was ready to bear any pain, hurt, or sorrow.

We were the perfect two, so in sync together,

With so much in common like birds of the same feather.

Somewhere down the road, the relationship started to stray

Causing a distance in communicating that appeared from day to day.

If only we could, turn back the hands of time, doing things differently, and happily ever after being mine.

I'm glad we're able to move on and agree we will still be friends, even though our new love should have been destined until the end.

ENTANGLED

I found myself entangled in a relationship brand new,

With nothing but good fortunes to only look forward to.

Something happened along the way; no one was accused,

It was as though a moment flashed and left me so confused.

It saddens me to think about how things went all wrong,

And now it's left me in a state where I feel so all alone.

Now it seems as though my mind will never be free,

Because the hurt and shame endured has become a part of me.

Yes, he shattered my world, all my hopes, and dreams,

Leaving me full of tears that flowed like endless streams.

I know I can't hide from the memories because day after day I've tried,

To find out not only am I entangled but to them, I'm also tied.

Yes, he did some awful things with wrongful intent no doubt,

Because deep inside, he already knew he didn't want to work it out.

I walk around trying to hide—all the misery I feel inside.

I do not know what the future holds, nor what's in store for me.

I only know that at this time, happiness I cannot see.

FLY FREE

As each day passes and a new one begins,

I find myself still at loose ends.

Caught up in a moment with thoughts of you,

wondering if you have these moments too...

Reminiscing on days of the past

and why our time together couldn't forever last.

Every since we've parted,

I've often felt kind of blue,

and every now and then,

I shed a tear or two.

But I won't be discouraged in trying to move on,

still remembering your smile, your touch, a song,

never forgetting what you meant to me,

and with that I'm able to let you FLY FREE!

STILL IN LOVE

Even though we've broken up and gone our separate way,

I still have these flashbacks that loving you is still okay.

I wished we had taken the time before our ship had sailed,

To try and figure out some things before the relationship failed.

We could have used our love, as strong as it seemed to be,

To see if we could get back what used to come easily.

But with it all, life's not always fair,

Doesn't mean that we didn't care.

One thing for sure I will always know,

I'm still in love, and that's fa' sho!

STILL MISSING YOU

Touching on a memory, one I do recall,

When I had you in my life and thought I had it all.

You touched me in a way no one ever has before,

You touched me in a way I've never wanted anyone more.

The thoughts of us I can't resist,

And your tender kiss I truly miss.

Remembering the things we used to do

And how much in love we were as two.

My days are sometimes still sad and blue,

But that's because I still miss you.

Even though we've parted and gone our separate way,

I still have these cherished memories that are forever here to stay!

TO ME

To me, you are like sunshine even when it rains,

And yes, we've had our share of a lot of hurt and pain.

To me, you are the path each day that I would walk,

Filling each step with just ordinary talk.

To me, you're like a song each day that I would sing,

Making sure each note has just the perfect ring.

To me, you're like cold water that quenches out a thirst,

To me, you're like the number one because it always comes first.

To me, you're like a flower that in its season will bloom,

To me, you're like a rhythm that carries its own tune.

This is my way of expressing what you mean to me,

Because to me, you're special, and that I hope you see!

SHARON THAMES

BEREAVEMENT

GRANDMA

A smooth, gentle breeze that's guided by the wind,

Grandma, that's what you were and also my special friend.

Always giving of your time,

Now that was nothing but true love divine.

Always there when needed, every time to take the call,

And not just for me, but Grandma, you were there for us all.

Now the time has come for you to be at rest,

Even though it hurt us, God knew what was best.

Grandma, we are going to miss you, with this there is no doubt,

But you can rest assured you'll always be talked about.

Rest in peace, Grandmother! We'll remember to keep a smile,

Knowing we'll see you again in just a little while!

HOW BEAUTIFUL

How beautiful are the flowers that grow in their array?

How beautiful is your smile you brighten us with every day?

How beautiful are the raindrops that fall from the sky?

How beautiful will it be now that we have to say goodbye?

How beautiful are the memories you left in our care?

How beautiful is it knowing that in our hearts, they will be there?

How beautiful will it be when we meet again?

When all the saints will gather, and we'll all say, Amen!

I CAN'T IMAGINE

It's hard to believe you've gone away,

I can't imagine life now, from day to day.

Longing to talk to you,

To laugh or tell a joke or two.

I can't imagine your life, now being null and void,

Wishing that turning back the hands of time, was just the pulling of a cord.

I can't imagine one day at a time, will now hold ever so true,

Because as each day passes by, I will be missing you.

I can't imagine life without you; things will never be the same,

But thank God for all the memories He allowed us to acclaim.

I can't imagine now when we look to the sky,

There will be your smile, shining bright and high.

Not imagining you're gone, but imagining when you look low,

There you will see without a doubt, the depth our love for you still show!

OUR BELOVED

The Lord has called our beloved home,

And now for a while, we shall moan.

The Lord is our shepherd, our rock, and our shield,

Only through Him will we heal.

You filled our lives with joy and tears,

Thank You, Jesus, for the years.

Now, beloved since you've gone away like dust that blows in the wind,

We know you're in a better place, where a new life will begin.

Like sand in an hourglass, like bark on the trees,

Your presence will be upon us, feeling like a cool winter breeze.

As we reminisce on days of the past,

There will be times of sadness, but it won't always last.

We will shed a tear or two but in a special way,

That's because of the cherished memories you left us every day.

We won't be discouraged; we'll be remembering your smile,

And how much you touched us with your own unique style.

You are already missed, never, ever forgotten, thought of and talked about, Because you are our dearly beloved, and in that, there is no doubt!

OUR BELOVED MOTHER

A few years have gone and come,

Since we lost you, Mom.

Your presence here no longer exists,

And you, our beloved, whom we truly miss.

Not a day goes past that we don't think of you,

And all the motherly things you used to do.

And one more thing to add a touch,

The grands miss you just as much!

It's true what they say about a loved one who dies,

It really affects everyone's lives.

Our days are sometimes still sad and blue but in a happy way,

Because even though you're gone, your memories are here to stay.

One more thing we added to this,

We sealed it with our love and a kiss!

HOLIDAYS

A FATHER'S DAY GREETING

What can be said about a father like you?

The role is understanding in everything you do.

You are classed as a hero because you always save the day,

And with each child, it's done in a different way.

You are supportive, loving through and through,

Being full of much wisdom that comforts when it's blue.

You are there when we need you and even when we don't,

And to let us down is something that you won't.

You're there in the smiles and there in the frowns,

There in the ups and always in the downs.

Fathers are not all biological; some are adopted in,

But by far it doesn't matter, they're still part of the trend.

Dad, this poem is written for you this Father's Day,

With a special kind of greeting with what we had to say!

HAPPY FATHER'S DAY

A MOTHER'S DAY POEM

(ESPECIALLY FOR YOU)

What can we say about a Mom like you?

Who gives of all her time,

Through all the struggles and despair, you still remain divine.

Full of joy and so much love,

Always putting family first and above.

Never complaining or dissatisfied,

Just there to listen or be a guide.

Willing to do whatever she can,

With open arms and extended hands,

Mom, we're your biggest fans.

The knowledge you give has so much conviction,

It imposes on our lives without a lot of restrictions.

All of the love and support you've shown,

Is what rooted us up as we have grown.

Mom, we hope your Mother's Day is special because you mean a lot,

And we want to say thank you for giving us all you've got!

HAPPY MOTHER'S DAY

BIRTHDAY WISHES

A BIRTHDAY WISH
FOR YOU

Today is one that's special; may all your dreams come true.

Today is like no other, for today belongs to you.

May it be surrounded by everything you love,

With all of God's great blessings, reigning from above.

May He continue to bless you with many more birthdays to come,

Making each one more special than the last ones.

May your health always flourish with the wisdom you will attain,

And may all the love bestowed in your heart, forever remain the same!

HAPPY BIRTHDAY
TO SOMEONE
SPECIAL

Today is a special day that only comes once a year,

A day that's filled with best wishes and lots and lots of cheer.

Coming from family, friends, and loved ones who hold you very dear.

A day of being pampered, doing things you like to do,

This day will also be filled with little surprises, too,

Letting you know this day is totally about you.

You will be covered in love that this day is sure to bring,

Because today, everything will have just the perfect ring.

Enjoy this day, best at will,

Because this is the day, you don't have to conceal!

HAPPY BIRTHDAY

REFLECTIONS

DADS

Dads are like heroes; they are there to save the day,

Making a safe haven so all will be okay.

They are the opposite of Moms,

But they, too, shelter you from any hurt or harm.

They are firm but tender,

Not easily to surrender.

They are supportive but protective,

And can be very objective.

They love you; they scold you,

But always ready to hold you.

When you are small, they seem to be your biggest obstacle,

And when you grow tall,

You will find they were no obstacle at all.

Dads give the best advice,

Most meaningful talks, not always nice.

They teach you to respect, stand tall, and be strong,

Don't always think you're never in the wrong.

They are leaders, but sometimes they stray,

Because they are human every day.

You learn to appreciate all they say and do,

And never have to question their depth of love for you.

MOMS

Moms are someone special who brings about a joy,

Because they're the first ones to experience the little girl or boy.

They love you through the good times; they love you through the bad,

They have that undying love like only Jesus had.

Moms love you dearly, and this you can always tell,

Because no matter what you do, on you, they will never bail.

They're there for you time and time again,

Even if it's just the holding of a hand.

You don't need lots of money to buy them a great gift,

They enjoy the little things because those bring about a lift,

And lets you know in a special way,

How much you always brighten their day!

A FRIEND IS

A friend is someone special; a friend is true to its name,

A friend is someone you tell everything,

And their loyalty remains the same.

A friend is someone you love and someone who loves you back.

Trust, honesty, and devotion is something they will not lack.

A friend is someone to laugh with and one to cry with, too,

Even in disagreement, they will still be there for you.

A friend is someone who will listen, whatever the case may be,

Never telling a single soul and never charging a fee.

A friend is someone who picks you up when you're feeling down,

Place your mind on other things to keep away the frown.

A friend is someone who appreciates the good in you and overlooks the bad,

Brings out the best in you like none you've ever had.

A friend is always there in your weakest time of need,

And you can rest assured the support is GUARANTEED!

ABOUT THE AUTHOR

Sharon Thames is kind, considerate, and loving in her own uniqueness. She enjoys bowling, movies, television dramas, and hanging out with family and friends. However, her passion is writing poetry. Sharon has always shown an interest in writing. She started writing poems at an early age, not realizing the talent developing within. Sharon has a natural way of expressing herself through words. She writes from her heart and soul. Sharon's poetry is intimate, soothing and consoling as it is written with lots of compassion. She gives all the glory to God because he always has her back!

www.ingramcontent.com/pod-product-compliance
Lightning Source LLC
LaVergne TN
LVHW040054090426
835513LV00028B/598